The Grass Is Greener in Your Own Backyard

by

Carla Newbern Thomas, M.D.

DORRANCE PUBLISHING CO., INC.
PITTSBURGH, PENNSYLVANIA 15222

ISBN #0-8059-5327-3
Printed in the United States of America

First Printing

For information or to order additional books, please write:
Dorrance Publishing Co., Inc.
643 Smithfield Street
Pittsburgh, Pennsylvania 15222
U.S.A.
1-800-788-7654
Or visit our web site and on-line catalog at *www.dorrancepublishing.com*

I dedicate this book to Cleo, Mom, Dad, Stephen, Carlton, Grandad, Nana, Tres, Phillips, Lucy, and Caleb.

Contents

Family Loyalty 1

The Gift of Life 3

One of Life's Greatest Sensations 5

The Haunted Attic 7

Sibling Rivalry 9

Simple Tasks 11

Climbing Mountains 13

The Quick One 15

The Price of Loquacity 17

The Importance of Trust 19

Success 21

Angel of the Flood 24

Harvest Fair Queen 26

How a Bully and a Crippled Child Became the Best of Friends 28

Win or Lose 30

Tetralogy of Fallot 31

Men Can Be Nurses, Too! 33

Trevor Shillito 35

Rabbits Are Not the Only Ones Who Need Rabbit Food 36

Running Deer 38

The Best Form of Health Insurance 40

A Doctor in the Hills 42

Crying Wolf 44

Who's Counting? 46

A Quest for the Key to the Lock 48

The Grass is Greener in Your Own Backyard .50

A New Companion 52

A Citation from the President 54

A Sharp Shooter 56

O Lord Jesus Christ 57

Blessed Beatitudes 58

Bless 59

Foxes Have Holes 61

I Believe in Miracles 62

Come on Board the Gospel Train 63

The Doctor of My Soul 64

The Books of the Holy Bible 65

Prophecies 66

Is Your Life a Mess or a Message 67

My Help Come from the Lord 68

Jesus Christ, the Light of Light 69

O Lord Our Lord 70

Adaptation: Mary Had a Little Lamb 72

Adaptation: Saints 73

My Soul Magnifies the Lord 74

Shepherd (Psalm 23) 75

Joyful Noise (Psalm 100) 76

The Lord Reigns (Psalm 93) 77

Family Loyalty

Toby was the seventh of twelve children. His parents had died five years ago in a car accident. His oldest brother and sister then took command of the Sugarbaker brood, though neither one of them had a job that could support twelve kids. All agreed that no matter how poor they became, each member should finish high school. Toby thought the idea was nice, but it did not put food on the table, warm a cold, crowded apartment, put clothes on his back, or pay the rent. That's when Toby became a heroin dealer.

With the extra income, he brought home meat, clothes for his baby sister, Cloteil, and brother, John, and paid half of the bills. Toby even had enough money to take his best friend, Fred, and girlfriend, Joan, out on dates. Toby kept his goods well hidden. Because he shared a room with Toby, only John knew about his business. When questioned by his suspicious older brothers and sisters, he replied he had an after-school job down on the wharf. With the comfort he provided, Toby deceived all of his family, except for John.

At the age of seventeen years, Toby Sugarbaker could peddle heroin to his neighbors more quickly than it was supplied to him. He was better at selling heroin than the oil company was at selling oil or than the water utility was at selling water. His addicted customers would rather have heroin than heat, water, or shelter. When they lost their jobs and could not support their habits, he forced them to steal. His addicted customers would rather have heroin than dignity or respect. He used his business acumen to poison the lives of those around him.

When his girlfriend left him for his best friend, he wanted vengeance. The next time Joan came for heroin, he gave her a different dose and then watched her as her breathing became slower and slower. She died of a heroin overdose. When Fred came for heroin, Toby supplied him with an old syringe as well. From the infected syringe, Fred contracted tetanus. He died the next day of lockjaw and tonic convulsions. John knew of these acts but kept quiet, lest Toby's anger be directed at him.

The baby, Cloteil, was loved by all. One day while cleaning John and Toby's room, she found some dirty syringes. When she went to dispose of them, one needle accidentally punctured her finger. She thought nothing of it but did mention the incident to John.

Over the next three months, Cloteil became very ill. At first her skin became yellow, including the whites of her dark brown eyes. Her joints began to ache and a rash erupted all over her body. On her right upper side

1

she developed pain and tenderness. John urged her to see a doctor but Cloteil refused. Toby was suspicious that she was on drugs. She denied any use but Toby did not believe her. He had seen this sickness too many times in his addicts. He knew she had hepatitis and would die unless hospitalized.

Cloteil's fever would not abate. When she developed large bruises over most of her body, she submitted to her family's request to go to the hospital. As they reached the hospital, Cloteil began to vomit blood. She lost consciousness. Though medicine was begun immediately, it was too late. Four months after pricking her finger with an infected needle, Cloteil was dead of hepatitis.

These three acts, which were related to Toby's business, enraged John. Two of the victims may have died anyway but his beloved sister had died needlessly, as an innocent bystander.

One night John brought three undercover policemen to see Toby at home.

"Toby Sugarbaker, you are under arrest for homicide and for the possession and distribution of heroin. You have the right to remain silent...." The policeman was interrupted by Toby.

"Officer, what is this about?" clamored Toby.

"I am turning you in to the police, Toby. I know where the heroin is and will give them all the details of the business," John replied.

"Why, John? Why have you forsaken me? Didn't I clothe you when you were naked, feed you when you were hungry, put a roof over your head, and protect you from hurt, harm, and danger?" Toby pleaded.

"Yes, you did, except you forgot to protect me from yourself. I saw how you hurt your best friends. I grieved over the harm done indirectly by you to Cloteil. I perceive you as a danger to the community and a poison to our family," John answered.

"I am your brother, John. Your blood brother! I love you. I grieved over Cloteil just like you. Do you think if Mom had been alive, she would like to see you doing this?" Toby's eyes were strained and his muscles tense. If he could lull John into thinking family loyalty was more precious and important than justice, then Toby had a chance at avoiding arrest. Only John could show the police where the goods were stored.

"Your love," John said with difficulty, "is worse than poison honey. The material comforts you gave us raised our social status but rotted our sense of self-respect. Mama always said, above all else, respect yourself and all life. You, who would dare to trick me into saving you by using family loyalty, have violated the first family law," John charged.

Toby failed at avoiding arrest. John handed over the goods and business books and later testified at the trial. At the end of the trial, Toby Sugarbaker received a sentence from the judge of imprisonment for life.

The Gift of Life

The Tarry twins were born on a typical hot, humid, Alabama day in the middle of a heat wave. Though Eric and Emil were identical twins, the similarity stopped there. As he grew, Eric sought to gain recognition, possessions, and power. Emil loved the land.

At twenty-three, they both married. Eric married a banker's daughter and had one son, Everett. Through political deals and bribes, he amassed great wealth. He planned to make Everett the next president of his corporation when he retired. He sent him to the best of schools, and he wore the latest dress suit fashions. They lived on the rich side of the railroad tracks. Eric was the envy of all. He boasted often to his twin. Yet Emil had never been one to be impressed, influenced, or controlled by Eric. For that reason alone, much strife arose between them.

Emil married a childhood sweetheart and took over his father's farm on the poor side of the railroad tracks. It was not that Emil endeavored to be poor but rather the richness he sought was in the conversion of poor soil to good soil by proper husbanding of the land. Until Alabama soil could be replenished, no money would be made in farming. He had three sons: Jeremiah, Jeff, and Tom. Tom, the youngest, was a sickly child who was physically deformed and required medical care Emil could not afford. Humbly he went to his brother Eric for assistance, but he was denied.

"We must pull ourselves up by our bootstraps," his twin retorted. When Tom died five years later, the bitterness deepened between the two families.

Although he had always been ruddy and robust, Everett was sixteen years old when he first noticed blood in his urine. He ignored it. On his annual visit to Dr. Smith, a urinalysis revealed blood and protein. His blood pressure also was dangerously elevated. By this time, even Everett admitted he was gravely ill. After several kidney studies, Dr. Smith concluded that Everett had a fatal kidney disease called "rapidly progressive glomerulonephritis." The cause was unknown. He would die unless he started dialysis or received a kidney from a compatible donor. Everett feared dialysis. Dialysis would mean being attached to a blood filtering machine which does the kidney's job for three days a week, four hours at a time, for the rest of his life. There would be a drastic change in his lifestyle, unless a compatible family member could donate a kidney. To be compatible meant a family member would have a similar set of genes to his own and no antibodies were present in the donor's blood which would attack his body cells. Unfortunately although his father, Eric, did have a similar set of genes, he also had antibodies which made him ineligible as a kidney donor for his only son. Eric became morose. He had always been able to buy all his son needed. Now the one thing he needed money could not buy. All hope seemed lost.

The tragedy of Everett Tarry spread through the county on both sides of the railroad tracks. Emil's son, Jeremiah, was saddened at this news. Remotely feeling he could help, he sought Dr. Smith without his father's knowledge. After performing several tests on Jeremiah, it was found that he was compatible as a donor. Like his Uncle Eric, Jeremiah had genes which were similar to Everett's. Unlike his uncle, however he had no antibodies which would attack Everett's cells.

"But what are genes?" Jeremiah asked.

"Genes are made of DNA, *d*eoxyribo*n*ucleic *a*cid. The genes one receives from his parents determine what he will look like. When genes are similar, it means that one person has a similar immune system to another. It is in this setting that an organ from one person can be transferred to another without rejection by the body. Both you, your father, and uncle have genes that are similar to Everett's. If your father and uncle had not been identical twins, these rare circumstances probably would not have occurred. It is better for Everett to receive a kidney from you than from his father because he, for some reason, has developed antibodies to Everett's cells. This means your uncle's immune system perceives Everett's cells as slightly foreign. Understand?"

"Yes. Thanks, Dr. Smith."

After obtaining consent from Emil, all agreed that Emil should be the one to announce the good news to Eric and his family. On Thanksgiving day, the Emil Tarry family went to visit the Eric Tarry family.

"My brother," Emil announced after a cheerless welcome from Eric, "I bring you good news. I bring you the gift of life. I have here evidence that Jeremiah can donate a kidney to your only son, in order that his life may be saved."

Eric was dumbfounded. Everett was ecstatic. There was silence as the twins viewed one another with expressions alternating between hate and love, confusion and understanding. Everett was the first to hug his outcast cousin, who was now casting hope for his future. Eric offered Emil his hand of thanks and reconciliation. Like wildfire on a dry, dusty day, the news spread throughout the countryside and on both sides of the railroad tracks that two brothers, once enemies, had been reunited through their sons.

One month later, Jeremiah donated a kidney to his cousin. In turn, Eric donated money to the local agricultural school and initiated a campaign to replenish the soil in the county. The two families became close. Thereafter, a great mutual respect arose between Eric and Emil Tarry.

4

One of Life's Greatest Sensations

For eleven years, Maria Tauber lived in the heart of the ghetto with her great-aunt, who was her last known relative. Her parents had died of tuberculosis during a severe winter before she was two years old. Her great-aunt Chelsey had taken care of her for these last nine years, but even she would not remain on earth for long. Three years ago, the doctors at the neighborhood health center found that she had widespread breast cancer. They told her she had a few years to live.

Maria did not fear the future. She figured any place would be better than the rat-infested, smog-dense, dimly lit, trash-filled, cold, over-crowded slum in which she lived. She was glad to leave when the social worker came to take her to a foster home after Aunt Chelsey passed away.

The new foster home was located on a farm where the Stone family lived. Mr. Stone was a farmer. Mrs. Stone made quilts. They had seven children, one of whom was Maria's age. Maria was delighted to be with them and they welcomed her into the family. This environment was so different from the one she had lived in for the past eleven years. The bright sunshine, green pastures, fresh well water, fast horses and fat, milk-laden cows were like a dream come true.

The Stone family was very concerned about Maria's state of health. They took her to the town doctor, Dr. Moyer. It didn't take long for Dr. Moyer to figure out the problem when he heard where Maria had come from and what she had been eating. During her physical exam, he found she had poorly formed teeth, mild curvature of the spine (scoliosis), a pigeon breast (prominent sternum), knobs on her ribs (which he called a rachitic rosary), bow legs, and knock knees.

"Mrs. Stone, this child has rickets. It is caused by a deficiency of vitamin D. We don't see this disease too much in this part of the country because the kids get plenty of sunshine and because mothers like you make it a habit to give them cod liver oil. An inactive form of vitamin D is stored in the skin. When the sunlight strikes the skin, it activates the vitamin D. Also, there is a high content of vitamin D in cod liver oil," explained Dr. Moyer.

"Well, with her doing outside chores on the farm and eating cod liver oil like the rest of my kids, she ought to get well in a hurry," exclaimed Mrs. Stone.

"You've got the right idea. Some of that fresh cow milk of yours would help too," added Dr. Moyer.

Maria did not realize how weak she had been until she became stronger on the Stone family diet. Best of all, she was given the chore of milking the cows and was allowed to drink as much of the milk as she wished. Truly one of life's greatest sensations was the feeling of morning-fresh, warm, sweet milk being sprayed into her mouth as she diverted the cow's teat upward toward the sun.

The Haunted Attic

Terra Nicole was five years old when she discovered she liked to eat the paint on the attic wall. Unlike the other rooms in their house, the attic had never been remodeled or repaired. Unlike the other members of her family, only Terra and her grandfather dared to enter the attic. Everyone else thought that it was haunted. Their house was of the Gothic style, built in the early eighteenth century. In the attic, her grandfather stored old clothes, furniture, and a collection of salt and pepper shakers. As a pullman porter (a person who works on a train), he had collected salt and pepper shakers from every city he visited. As an excuse to go to the attic, Terra Nicole said she wanted to see the collection. At first she ate very little paint. As she ate more, it became sweet to her. She had to have it every day.

After three months of eating paint, Terra Nicole began to have abdominal cramps, general weakness, dizzy spells, and tingling toes and fingers. Her grandfather noticed that her color "wasn't right." Concerned, her grandfather took her to the doctor. He told Dr. Thomas that, "She has become so skinny and sickly. Her color isn't right. She isn't as vibrant as she is supposed to be. Plus, although I tell her to brush her teeth vigorously, she has developed a black line around her gums. What does all this mean, Dr. Thomas?" He waited while Dr. Thomas examined Terra Nicole.

"Well, Mr. Nelson," gravely spoke Dr. Thomas, "your granddaughter has been poisoned accidentally by lead. All of these symptoms and signs point to chronic lead poisoning, or what we call plumbism. In order to cure the illness, we need to find the source of the lead Terra Nicole has been eating. Terra, do you understand what we are talking about?"

"Yes," answered Terra.

"Have you been painting with some very old paint?"

"No."

"Have you been drinking moonshine, meaning illegal jack-leg liquor?" asked Dr. Thomas.

"No ma'am, Dr. Thomas," answered Terra Nicole.

"Mr. Nelson, do you have moonshine available in the house?"

"No, Dr. Thomas," replied Mr. Nelson.

"Terra Nicole, have you been eating paint off of the wall anywhere in your house?" questioned Dr. Thomas carefully.

Proudly interrupting, Mr. Nelson boasted, "Dr. Thomas, I know she has not been eating old paint. I give the house a fresh coat of paint every five years. It's the best painted house in the neighborhood."

"Mr. Nelson, where do you live?"

"On Judith's Fancy."

"That's a very old neighborhood, isn't it? It's one of the oldest in the city. Does it have a basement or attic?" she queried.

"Yes, why I forgot all about that attic. Terra Nicole likes to visit the attic in order to see my salt and pepper shaker collection," Mr. Nelson remembered.

"Do you also paint this attic?"

"Uh, no, Dr. Thomas. Matter of fact, I have never remodeled or repaired it."

"Are its walls painted?"

"Why, yes. But the paint has peeled and crumbled over the years."

Terra Nicole interrupted, "Granddad, is it wrong for me to eat that paint? It tastes sort of sweet. I eat it all the time."

"That's the answer. I bet that old paint you are eating contains lead. The newer paint used in today's homes doesn't contain the lead that older paint has. Terra Nicole, I am going to give you a medicine which will help eliminate the lead from your body. Until you get better, you will have to be hospitalized," announced Dr. Thomas.

"Dr. Thomas, which parts of her body are most affected?"

"Lead generally is deposited in the bones, liver, kidneys, brain, muscles, gums, and intestines."

"Thanks, Dr. Thomas. We sure are grateful Terra Nicole is going to recover. Meanwhile I'll remodel the attic and give it a fresh coat of paint. Maybe that way her friends won't feel the attic is haunted. After it's repaired, everyone will be able to view the salt and pepper shaker collection," beamed Mr. Nelson. "Sound all right with you, Terra Nicole?"

"Sure, Granddad. I think I'll stick to food whenever I get hungry again."

Sibling Rivalry

Joel and Allen Truman were siblings but they were also each other's archrival in everything, especially wrestling.

On one New Year's eve, Mr. and Mrs. Truman decided they would go next door to visit their neighbors. Since it would only be for a short while, they felt it was all right to leave their sons at home alone. Joel was eleven years old and Allen was twelve. Before leaving, Mr. Truman gave strict orders of no fighting.

While they were gone, Joel and Allen wrestled more vigorously than usual. Although Joel was able to pin his older brother several times, he also received several blunt abdominal blows in the process. Both agreed not to tell their parents about this activity since neither was hurt very badly.

About one month later, Joel became very weak and pale. He vomited every morning. Mrs. Truman found he had a fever. At first, she thought that Joel had a cold. However after three weeks, when the cold did not improve and small bluish-black blotches appeared over Joel's body, Mrs. Truman took him to the doctor immediately.

After taking a history and physical exam, Dr. Grove felt lab studies were in order to obtain the correct diagnosis. A smear of Joel's blood showed many white blood cells. A bone marrow study showed the same. After consultation with other doctors, Dr. Grove told the Trumans that Joel had acute lymphocytic leukemia. In order to fight the disease, he would need chemotherapy and radiation. His prognosis was poor. Joel accepted his diagnosis as his cross to bear in life. Studies showed Allen could donate his bone marrow to help Joel. This act of compassion eased Joel's suffering. Joel died six months later but he knew Allen was a true brother and not a rival because he had suffered for him.

Meanwhile Allen became very depressed after hearing the news of his brother. Neither the doctor nor his parents had adequately explained to him what was happening to his younger brother. Consequently Allen felt it was his fault that Joel had become ill. He felt sure that those wrestling blows he had given Joel one month ago had caused the leukemia. In order to punish himself, Allen decided to stop eating.

At first his parents did not notice. Soon, however, Mrs. Truman noted that in two weeks Allen had lost ten pounds. Nothing she could cook, say, or do would make Allen eat. She took him to see Dr. Grove.

After consulting with a psychiatrist, Dr. Grove told the Trumans that Allen was suffering from anorexia nervosa. Anorexia nervosa is a psychiatric disorder in which a person voluntarily stops eating and suffers severe weight loss. It is usually difficult to cure, but Dr. Grove was very astute. He had known Allen since his birth and had never detected any mental illness. He made an educated guess that Allen's mental disturbance was a reaction to Joel's illness.

Dr. Grove took Allen aside and spoke to him for a long time. He asked Allen how he felt about Joel's illness.

"I think it is my fault," Allen cried. "It is my fault because I kicked Joel in the abdomen two months ago. He has leukemia because I kicked him."

"Allen, I am sorry you had to suffer like this," Dr. Grove answered. "You should understand that the leukemia Joel has was not caused by you. If leukemia occurred whenever two brothers wrestled, then almost every American family would have it. Let me explain leukemia. In your blood there are red blood cells (RBCs) which carry oxygen to cells, platelets which help to clot blood when needed, and white blood cells (WBCs) which fight infection. These cells come from the inner parts of bone which is called bone marrow. WBCs are the soldiers of the body. Joel's WBCs, or soldiers, do not grow, develop, or function as they should. These kind of WCBs grow uncontrolled. They occupy most of the bone marrow and blood. Joel has leukemia. 'Leuki' refers to the WBC and 'emia' refers to the blood. The cause of leukemia is not completely known.

Scientists are looking for cures. Whether you had wrestled with Joel or not, he would have become ill. You did not cause his leukemia. Do you feel better?"

"Yes, Dr. Grove. Thank you for the explanation."

Relieved that he was not the cause of his brother's illness, Allen decided to stop punishing himself and start eating. He began to gain weight and grow healthy. Instead of wrestling, Allen and Joel accompanied Mr. Truman to wrestling matches at the new professional sports complex downtown. Until Joel died six months later, Allen was able to provide strong support for him. Even as Allen was his archrival, so he became his best friend.

Simple Tasks

Sari was a very busy, affable person. At the age of fourteen, he had places to go, people to see, appointments to keep, and many things to do. As a dreamer of big complex plans, he had little time for simple tasks. He preferred to read an extra chapter in his book on computer languages rather than tidy his room. He thought it was more worthy to attend a club meeting than to rake the leaves in the yard. To him, it was more esthetically pleasing to perfect his saxophone technique than to take out the trash. One particular simple task Sari disliked was taking time out every day to have a good bowel movement. The smell was disgusting. The pain was agonizing. The muddy-brown, algae-green appearance of feces was revolting. As much as possible, he skipped his bowel movements. He did not realize his mistake.

All simple tasks have a purpose. They are essential to the smooth functioning of any process. When they are omitted nothing may happen in the short run; but in the long run, much havoc is wrought. This fact is illustrated by the adage, "A stitch in time saves nine." In a literal sense, it means that one poorly sewn stitch may cause you to have to sew nine extra stitches to correct the mistake. Sewing poorly may take nine-fold as much time as sewing correctly in the first place. Sari was to learn this lesson the hard way.

One morning Sari noticed that there was a sharp pain in the right lower quadrant of his abdomen:

The sharp pain was constant. It was associated with frequent cramps, nausea, and later, vomiting (emesis). It was worsened by eating and walking. Sari had forgotten he had not moved his bowels for seven days.

As this had never happened to Sari before, he became afraid and told his mom. Also concerned, his mom took him to the doctor's office. After examining him, Dr. Asdof said, "Sari, based on the history you have told me and your physical examination, I think primarily you are constipated. However, I cannot rule out appendicitis. You will have to go to the hospital. We will observe you there. We will help you to have a bowel movement. If your pain worsens, then in the morning we may have to perform an appendectomy. Appendicitis means inflammation of the appendix. Appendectomy refers to the removal of the appendix. 'Append' means 'to hang' in Latin. The appendix is a wormlike, blind vestigial structure which hangs off of the large bowel. It is located at the junction of the small intestines and the large bowel."

Sari's mom then asked, "How much will this cost?"

"Well, I estimate that for each day he spends in the hospital, it will cost at least three hundred dollars," said Dr. Asdof.

"Wow, that is more than all the allowance I receive in a year," exclaimed Sari.

"Thank you, Dr. Asdof. We will go straight to the hospital," said his mother sternly.

Fortunately, after three enemas, Sari had the biggest bowel movement in his life. To his amazement, the pain disappeared immediately. Surgery was obviated. In the morning, he went home.

He had learned a lesson the hard and expensive way. From now on he would perform simple tasks without delay, especially those concerning his body.

Climbing Mountains

When Andrea Leonard was four months old, her mother found that when she kissed her, the taste of salt was left upon her lips. She also noted that after a vigorous cry, a line of brine above her brow appeared. She called Dr. Taylor, who requested that Andrea come for a visit.

"Mrs. Leonard, have other members of your family had this trait of tasting like salt?" inquired Dr. Taylor.

"No, but you should know, Andrea was adopted. We know nothing of her past history."

"Since she has been with you, has she been gaining weight appropriately?"

"Well, doctor, matter of fact, she has lost weight since coming to us one month ago. I thought she was adjusting to the environment and my cooking. Thus far, she does not like the variety of baby food I serve, although I have switched brands three times and added vitamins to her diet. Her stools are yellowish and smell worse than mine. Her belly has become protuberant and firm, while her muscles are very thin. She looks like the starved children one sees on those commercials for CARE."

"What about colds?" asked Dr. Taylor.

"Curious you should ask. She has had a bad chest cold and runny nose since she came. That daughter of mine is a regular mucous factory."

"I need to do some more tests before I can say for sure what is ailing Andrea. I need to analyze her sweat, saliva, sputum, and stool."

After awhile, Dr. Taylor invited Mrs. Leonard back to his office.

"Mrs. Leonard, your baby has a serious congenital disease called cystic fibrosis. It is hereditary, meaning it runs in families, and its cause is unknown. About ninety-five percent of the people who contract the disease are white. Cystic fibrosis is a disease in which there is a disturbance of what we call exocrine glands. Examples of these are salivary glands, the pancreas, sweat glands, and mucous secreting cells in the lungs. In the sweat glands this disturbance is manifest as an inability to lower the salt content of sweat. This is why your baby tastes salty. In the pancreas, fibrocystic structures distort the normal architecture. This causes the pancreas to be deficient in enzyme production. When there are not enough enzymes being secreted into the intestines, then one cannot absorb food—no matter what brand you buy. This is why Andrea is not gaining weight. Your cooking is not the cause of Andrea's malnutrition. Furthermore, the malodorous stool she has is mainly caused by undigested fats. Understand?"

"Yes, Dr. Taylor. How long will she live, since there is no cure for cystic fibrosis?"

"Some people live until their teenage years, others die in infancy. Although we have no cure, we do have ways of ameliorating, meaning making less harsh, the effects of the disease. Since a cure may be discovered any day, I cannot predict how long Andrea will live."

"Dr. Taylor, what will we do now?"

"I need to hospitalize her in order to find which medicines will help her and to help her gain weight more quickly, using a technique called parenteral nutrition. Parenteral nutrition means that through a tube placed in a vein, we give her the protein, carbohydrates, fats, and vitamins she needs for growth and development."

"You mean you put food directly in the blood?" exclaimed Mrs. Leonard.

"No, not exactly. Actually, we infuse the breakdown products, or what you can call the building blocks, of protein, carbohydrates, and fats. We chemically do the job that her intestines normally perform."

"Will she ever eat again?"

"Yes. She will have parenteral nutrition only for a short while. Then she will switch to a full diet but the new medicines will help her to digest food better. Also while in the hospital, we will treat her respiratory infection.

"Above all, do not despair nor feel guilty. Andrea needs you, your love, and support. All of us are born with mountains in the horizon of life which we must climb. All of us are born with the capability of climbing those mountains. Remember Helen Keller. Remember President Franklin D. Roosevelt. Though I shall be with you all the way, you must never lose hope. For to lose hope is to fail to climb even the mole hill."

The Quick One

Tai Sue Ching and her family came from Chinju. Chinju is a city of 77,000 people in South Korea. The main business in Chinju is cotton. After the Korean war, the Chings migrated to California to seek a better life.

Mr. Ching was good with his hands and worked as a carpenter. Mrs. Ching kept children during the day, along with her own eight kids. Tai Ching was the oldest daughter.

Tai enjoyed children and took an active role in the education of her brothers and sisters. It was fascinating to watch each one as he or she was born and then learned to walk and talk and then learned to read and write. Most of all, watching a birth intrigued Tai. She decided after high school she would become a midwife. A midwife is a nurse who is licensed to assist a mother in birth. Yet as fate would have it, Tai would have to deliver a baby before she became a midwife.

On the night of January 10, Tai's pregnant mother began having labor pains. An hour and a half later, the bag of waters surrounding the baby broke. This sign meant the baby would be born soon. As usual, they called the midwife, who had delivered her first eight children. The midwife said that she would come after awhile. She had to attend first to Mrs. Lee, who was surely going to give birth within the hour.

The Chings were satisfied with these arrangements. Although Tai was not a midwife, she had seen her seven brothers and sisters born. She knew exactly what to do just in case the midwife arrived too late.

During the next thirty minutes, Tai was certain the baby was already in the second stage of labor because she could see the top of the baby's head. She checked to make sure the baby was positioned in the correct manner. She found that everything was all right. The baby had descended from the womb to the birth canal.

When Mrs. Ching approached the third hour of labor, the midwife still had not arrived. Her contractions became very strong.

"Tai, you have seen the midwife deliver babies many times. I can wait no longer. You must deliver the baby."

"All right mom. I'll go clean my hands. Everything else is ready."

At the stroke of midnight, the ninth Ching child was born. When the baby's head emerged from between her mother's legs, Tai gently but quickly pulled the baby out.

"It's a boy," she announced to the family and gave him to her mother.

15

She clamped the umbilical cord. Through the umbilical cord, the baby had received nourishment from his mother. The umbilical cord was attached to her by means of the placenta. The placenta is located at the junction between the umbilical cord and uterus. The uterus is called the womb. It is a very muscular female organ. It contracts during labor to expel the baby from the uterus into the vagina, which is the birthing canal. When the baby emerges from the vagina, he begins to breathe.

After fifteen more minutes, the placenta separated from the uterus and was also expelled. The birth was over.

They called the midwife at Mrs. Lee's house. Mrs. Lee had not given birth yet. The midwife was glad all had gone well. She would come soon to check the baby.

In honor of her role in the birth of the ninth child, the family let Tai name him. After careful thought, she named him Hua Sprague Ching. Hua Ching was named after his grandfather. Because he was born so quickly, Tai made his middle name Sprague, which means "the quick one."

The Price of Loquacity

"Kelly! Come down. Our company has arrived," her mother shouted from the bottom of the steps. Lazily, fifteen-year-old Kelly drifted back from her daydreams to finish snapping the bone-colored buttons of her new blue dress. Today some cousins whom she had never met were coming for dinner. She had been told that her Uncle Henning was a thinly built, reticent sort of chap who was not much for conversation. Her Aunt Sally, in contrast, was a strong, stocky woman who was loquacious and loved to eat. They had a son and daughter named Raymond and Edmonia. Of Raymond it was said that he could add numbers as quickly as a computer. Edmonia was known for her talents of playing the violin and piano. Everyone thought she was a child prodigy, just like Mozart.

Kelly descended the steps to be enveloped by arms and kisses. Surely this evening promised to be fun and full of joviality.

As Kelly predicted, Aunt Sally dominated the dinner conversation from the appetizer on with tales of their youth. When she ceased to speak, all was quiet for a brief moment. It seemed that her ears would at last enjoy silence. Her hope was dashed as Aunt Sally began to survey her features.

"Kelly, do you have a boyfriend?" Aunt Sally queried. Kelly disliked adults peering into her social life. "Kelly, it's about time you took a fancy to some of those handsome young men. My, my, my. When I was your age, I dated plenty of young men," continued Aunt Sally.

Uncle Henning, who had refrained from participating in the conversation thus far, interjected, "Sally, must you always paint a rosy picture of the past? When I met you, you were suave and debonair, but all of those guys were surely losers. I am the best thing that ever happened to you." While everyone laughed uproariously, Aunt Sally and Uncle Henning exchanged enigmatic glances only those who knew their past could decipher.

As Aunt Sally chewed what seemed to Kelly to be too much steak at one time, she mused, "You're right, Henning. All that glitters ain't gold, as the old folks used to say."

But Aunt Sally was not smiling. Instead a great trepidation possessed her. Her face became contorted. Then she grabbed her throat. Explosively, she choked. Everyone was frozen with fear, except for Kelly. Kelly sprang from her chair. Quickly placing her arm on Aunt Sally's chest, she bent her over applied four back blows. Then she encircled her waist above the navel and gave four upward abdominal thrusts. Aunt Sally still coughed violently.

Rapidly she repeated the procedure for rescuing a choking person: four back blows followed by four abdominal thrusts. On the fourth thrust, a large chunk of steak was ejected from her mouth and the coughing ceased. There was silence and relief.

Patting her on the back, her father said, "Kelly, I'm proud of you. Just think, if you had not taken that Red Cross first aid course, Aunt Sally could have died from suffocation."

Aunt Sally embraced her. "Thank you. I owe my life to you."

The Importance of Trust

When Cora Delaney was sixteen years old, her mother urged her to see a gynecologist to make sure she was developing properly. The gynecologist is a doctor who specializes in health care for women. It is a good idea for a woman to see a gynecologist at least once while she is in good health. Thinking her adolescent daughter would be delighted to do something that adults do, Mrs. Delaney met with some disappointment when Cora refused to go.

"But why, Cora?" exclaimed Mrs. Delaney.

"My friends say the exam is dehumanizing, painful, and embarrassing. Mama, I'm afraid."

"Listen, honey, President Roosevelt once said, 'There is nothing to fear except fear itself.' I'll go with you to allay your fears. If you're calm and relaxed, there is only minimal discomfort. Let me tell you what will happen. After taking your vital signs such as pulse and blood pressure, the doctor will examine your breasts and then do an internal exam to check your vagina, uterus, and ovaries.

If you want, we can go to see that new lady gynecologist, Dr. Bertha Albee. Besides, who are you going to trust? Me, who raised you and has known you all your life, or your friends, who are no wiser than you?"

"Okay, Mama. I'll give it a try," resigned Cora.

On Monday, they went to see Dr. Albee. Soft-spoken and friendly but professional, Dr. Albee and Cora liked each other from the start. Mrs. Delaney was pleased that Dr. Albee could so effortlessly put Cora at ease. By explaining everything she was going to do, the exam was completed with minimal discomfort. While Cora was dressing, Dr. Albee spoke with Mrs. Delaney.

"Mrs. Delaney, your daughter is basically healthy except for one detail. Her right ovary is twice as large as the left. I would like to do further studies, although I have a good idea as to what the mass is."

"Dr. Albee, Cora has been healthy all her life. How could this happen? Can she still have children? Does she have...cancer?" she nervously asked.

"I suspect but cannot confirm at this stage that her left ovary is normal, and that she will be able to have children in the future. It is possible that there is a benign growth on the right ovary. I would like to get an x-ray of her abdomen, a sonogram which uses sonar waves to define internal structures, an intravenous pyelogram, which outlines the urinary system and a barium enema, which outlines the large bowel. Because the ovaries lie in proximity to the large bowel and urinary structures, I need to see if the mass is affecting these structures."

"Dr. Albee, I forbid you tell my daughter she is going to die of cancer."

"Please, Mrs. Delaney, collect yourself. First of all, the prognosis for Cora is very good. She is young, healthy and has a will to live. Second of all, I do not know yet what exactly Cora has. It may be a tumor or it may be a benign cyst which will disappear in a few months. Third of all, trust is very important and vital to a relationship. In my experience, sooner or later patients figure out what diagnosis they carry. I prefer to avoid deception and reveal the truth in a manner the patient can understand from the beginning. Please, Mrs. Delaney, **don't put me in this position**. Only if I have her trust will I, in a time of crisis, be the support she needs!" Dr. Albee ceased because Mrs. Delaney was on the verge of tears.

"What is it, Mrs. Delaney?"

"I feel guilty because I lied to Cora. I made her come in because I thought she was pregnant. I told her she was coming for a regular check-up. I have not trusted her since she started dating a young man I did not like. Now you tell me she is going to die of cancer or be sterile."

"Mrs. Delaney, I have said no such thing. Since she has had regular periods there is a very good chance she is fertile. Forget the reason you came for today. Don't feel guilty; even mothers make mistakes. Let us hope for the best, prepare for the worst, and maintain a trusting, open relationship. Okay?"

"Okay. You can tell her."

Dr. Albee told Cora in a simple way of her mass. To her mother's relief, Cora received the information with equanimity. During the operation, a dermoid cyst was found on the right ovary and removed. Her left ovary was normal. During her uneventful convalescence, Cora and Mrs. Delaney became close and began to express true feelings about their conflicts. Their relationship had been strengthened in crisis. Cora learned that good health care meant going to see a doctor regularly, whether one is ill or well. Cora's mother learned that a relationship built on lies imprisons one in guilt. Thus the truth set her free.

Success

At the age of twenty, Solomon Clemmons was sure that his wisdom in the business world, in the next three years, place his growing company among the first five hundred that *Fortune* magazine thought were the most successful in America. Every obstacle heretofore encountered he had overcome with his strong will and determination. He had finished high school at sixteen. He finished college at eighteen. He finished business school six months ago.

One of his best friends was Professor Jay T. Donoho at the business school. He had chosen Solomon as his protégé. Solomon felt the professor had helped him to develop his potential to the fullest.

When his business in Persian rugs was six months old, Solomon noticed he had developed exquisitely tender red nodules on his extremities and had lost ten pounds for no apparent reason, other than the stress associated with his executive position. Two months later he developed a low, right-sided, steady discomfort which was associated with abdominal fullness, fatigue, and occasional vomiting. Concerned, he examined his stool. He found it to be foul smelling and brownish-yellow in color with sparse speckles of blood clots.

There was a list of many things in the world Solomon would not tolerate, like slovenliness and tardiness; blood was at the top of this list. He made an appointment to see his doctor the next week, after he returned from a business trip in Persia.

In Persia, Solomon developed a low-grade fever, increased lower right-sided crampy pain and, to his alarm, pneumaturia. Pneumaturia is the passing of air with urine when one urinates. The Persian doctors thought that possibly he had contracted one of the local infectious diseases and he should seek medical care immediately upon reaching America.

After his visit to Dr. Martin, Solomon underwent several digestive and urinary tract tests. He returned to see Dr. Martin, who informed him that, "According to the history, physical exam, and tests, I feel you have Crohn's disease or what is also known as regional enteritis, Solomon."

"How did I acquire it, Dr. Martin?"

"The cause is unknown; we suspect it is either familial, infectious, or immune."

"Dr. Martin, how many people are prone to it?"

"About two to three people for every 100,000 Americans acquire the disease each year. Jews are three times as likely to be affected as non-Jews. It tends to attack people in the fifteen to thirty-five year age range."

"Can you explain more clearly what it is, please?"

"Sure, Solomon. Regional enteritis is a chronic inflammatory disease in which parts of the small intestines and sometimes the large bowel become swollen, irritated, and easily bleed. This swelling obstructs the passage of stool. That explains the kind of diarrhea you have. Associated with Crohn's disease are the red nodules on your legs as well as poor absorption of food. The latter is why you lost weight. Because the urinary and digestive systems are contiguous, meaning that they lie close together, inflammation in one can spread to the other. When this happens, a tunnel or what we call fistula, can form. You passed air with urine because a fistula between your digestive and urinary tracts allowed air in the digestive tract to cross over into the urinary tract. The air was expelled when you passed urine. Understand?"

"Yes, Dr. Martin. What will happen next?"

"You will need surgery to correct the fistula. Then we will treat you with medicines. If medicines fail, then surgery is indicated," said Dr. Martin gravely.

On his medicines, Solomon felt better but resented his illness because he could find no cure. This was the first obstacle in his life he could not remove. He went to see Professor Donoho.

After hearing Solomon's history, Professor Donoho surprised him by saying, "This illness may be good for you."

Solomon measured the wine bottle. One glass of wine usually did not provoke such preposterous statements from his friend.

"Solomon, all your life you have solved problems by removing them. Unlike a blackboard, life sometimes presents us with problems that cannot be erased or removed. Through your wisdom, you have been able to remove problems. Yet you lack one thing— serenity. With serenity, one finds the strength to live with problems that cannot be removed. When one combines wisdom and serenity, then there exists a balance called equanimity. In your pursuits, you have sought, achieved, and expected success. Failure does not even exist in your vocabulary. You view yourself to be no less God-like than Alexander the Great."

"But surely we are taught to seek perfection, prosperity, and honor. What is wrong with that?" Solomon demanded.

"That is fine, except when you go so far as to become attached and emotionally dependent upon these things, you also become vulnerable to self-destructive resentment when unavoidable illness, sorrow, or disgrace enter your life. Listen, Meister Eckhart, a German philosopher, once said, 'True detachment means a mind as little moved by what befalls, by joy and sorrow, honor and disgrace, as a broad mountain by a gentle breeze. Such motionless detachment makes a man superlatively God-like.' Understand?"

"I think I see what you mean, Professor Donoho. Success is based on an ability to achieve as well as an ability to weather failure," Solomon concluded triumphantly.

Thereafter Solomon was able to take his illness in stride. He continued to work hard, without resentment. Five years later, his company was listed among the first five hundred in *Fortune* magazine as one of the most successful in the country.

Angel of the Flood

At the age of fifteen, Jessica and her family were homeless because of a large flood. Her father had used the family savings to build what was their dream house overlooking the river. Now that same river had overwhelmed and taken their home down the river, never to be seen again. Not even her nightmares had ever been this bad. Life was unpredictable. Today they were homeless; yesterday they had lived in the prettiest house on the block. What would tomorrow bring? Yet Jessica was thankful. Except for some small cuts, bruises, and sprains, every one in her family had escaped unharmed. Other families had not been as fortunate.

Jessica wondered, how would she attend school or go on a date without clothes? How would they eat? Surely they could not visit neighbors up in the hills for long before wearing out their welcome. All these questions she posed to the rescue worker in charge of their group. Her name was Maud Stenson.

"Maud," Jessica inquired, "how will our family be taken care of?"

"The Red Cross will help your family to get back on its feet and return to normal as soon as possible. We will take care of your immediate medical needs, give you a shelter temporarily, and provide a few clothes," answered Maud in a hopeful manner.

Maud intrigued Jessica. She was cheerful and tended to dispel the gloom of victims in her charge. Jessica figured she must have been paid to come provide relief for flood victims at this hour in the morning. She dared to ask her salary.

"Maud, how much are you paid to do this sort of work?" Jessica asked.

"Oh dear, I am not paid. This is volunteer work. I am a nurse at the Shady Rest Nursing Home," she replied.

"When did you first volunteer?"

"Thirty years ago."

"Thirty years ago!" Jessica exclaimed. "When did the Red Cross begin?"

"Well, it's a long story. Care to sit down?"

"Sure." Jessica sat in attention.

"Curiously enough, the Red Cross is not an American invention," Maud began. "A man named Jean Henri Dunant organized the International Red Cross in Europe in 1864. So moved was Clara Barton by the aid provided by the Red Cross for the wounded in the Franco-Prussian war that she organized the American Red Cross in 1881."

"What kind of person was Clara Barton?" Jessica inquired.

"Clara Barton was an extraordinary and generous woman. She lived from 1821 to 1912. She was born on Christmas Day in a small New England town. At the age of fifteen, she became a teacher and then went on to be a government clerk, lecturer, relief organizer, and battlefield heroine. During the Civil War, she broke tradition and worked on the front lines of battle in order to provide care for the Union's wounded soldiers. Because the government treasury was low, she often donated money from her own funds to pay for the first aid supplies she needed. To the soldiers, she was known as the 'angel of the battlefield'." Maud drew her speech to a close. She was being called to help other flood victims.

"Jessica, I must go. Will you be all right?"

"Yes, Maud. But there's one thing I would like to say. Having watched you administer aid to everyone here, I think that if Clara Barton was called 'angel of the battlefield', you ought to be called 'angel of the flood'. Maybe one day I will be a volunteer, too. Thank you for the care we have received," said Jessica earnestly.

"Perhaps when your family becomes situated again, you can volunteer at the hospital or nursing home. You will find it is more worthy to give than to receive."

Harvest Fair Queen

"I am the perfect beauty," Mae Larson whispered as she peered in the mirror at herself. "I have the skin, curves, height, and weight women dream of and men fight wars for. Only I can be the choice for Harvest Fair Queen this year. The judges can't possibly feel anyone else comes close to my perfect beauty."

Mae Larson attempted to allay her fears by giving herself this speech. She used to believe wholeheartedly she was a perfect beauty until this morning. While shaving her underarms, she noticed her left breast looked different from the right breast. When she examined herself carefully, she found a small, discrete, rubbery, smooth, movable lump about the size of her finger tip. She decided it would go away if she ignored it.

Three months later, her mother took her to the doctor for her annual physical check-up. Frantic that Dr. Chalter would discover her lump, Mae created excuses not to go. However her mother was determined she go. After the exam, Dr. Chalter called them both into her office.

"Mae, you are basically healthy except for one detail. You have a small breast lump which you neglected to tell me about earlier. How long has it been there?" she asked in a gentle manner.

"Three months at least, Dr. Chalter. It seems to grow during my periods, then it becomes small again," admitted Mae.

"Yes, from all the evidence I have seen thus far, I think you have a common benign growth called fibroadenoma."

"Dr. Chalter," asked Mrs. Larson, "will she live? Can it be cured?"

"Yes, she has a good chance to live and to be cured, if we do an operation."

"But Dr. Chalter," cried Mae, "I am perfect. If you take away my breast, I will be ugly."

"Mae, calm down. First of all," counseled Dr. Chalter, "the fibroadenoma is very small. With the latest surgical techniques, a small, barely visible, three-centimeter scar line is all you will notice after the surgeon excises the lump. We will not be taking away your breast. Second of all, I hope that one day you realize beauty comes from the inside, not the outside. One can be known as ugly though she is a perfect physical beauty. In contrast, one can be known as beautiful, though she lacks attractive features. Reflect on this, Mae. I will schedule your surgery for one week from today, if that is convenient."

"Yes, Dr. Chalter," answered the Larsons, "that's fine."

While recovering from surgery, Mae had much time for reflection on the meaning of perfection and beauty. One afternoon, Jim Kelly, her boyfriend, came to visit.

"Hi, Jim."

"Hi, Mae. Look, I brought roses for you."

"They smell very nice. Thank you, Jim."

"You seem sad. How did it go?" Jim inquired.

"Fine. I have been thinking about my reputation of being a perfect beauty. When the word gets around about my operation, no one will believe I am the perfect beauty anymore. Furthermore, I am surprised to see you today. I figured you would leave me unless I was more beautiful than any other woman. Have you come to say goodbye?"

"No, Mae. I have not come to say goodbye."

After a long silence during which they held hands, Jim began, "Mae, sometimes I wish I were blind."

"Why, Jim?" said Mae anxiously.

"Because if I were blind and still your boyfriend, then you would realize I love the total you—mind, body, and soul, not just the outer covering. We have been reading Kahlil Gibran lately in philosophy class. He says that beauty '...is not the image you would see nor the song you would hear, but rather an image you see though you close your eyes and a song you hear though you shut your ears....' Isn't that the truth? Isn't that the true meaning of beauty?" asked Jim as he looked into her eyes, searching for some sign of understanding.

"You mean, even if I were not the Harvest Fair Queen, you would want me?" asked Mae incredulously.

"Yes, Mae. Other girls don't matter to me. That's why I don't compare them to you. I love you for being you," Jim confessed.

Mae was speechless. All this time she had been a contestant in a beauty rat race, little realizing that even if she finished first, she would still be a rat.

"Mae, learn to trust me, then you won't be insecure."

Mae was noticeably a different person when she returned to school. Because she no longer saw girls as competitors, she found it easier to make friends. She found life itself was beautiful, even if you weren't the Harvest Fair Queen.

How a Bully and a Crippled Child Became the Best of Friends

To take advantage of the new job opportunities in Alaska, the Castillo family moved to a small community on the outskirts of Anchorage. Mr. and Mrs. Castillo were engineers and assisted in the planning of the Alaskan pipeline. Maria, age twelve, and Miguel, age sixteen, went to the nearby high school. The Castillos were sure Maria would fare well in this new environment; but for Miguel, who had cerebral palsy, they had strong reservations about his learning, well-being, and safety. When Miguel was born, it was found that his umbilical cord had been wrapped four times around his neck. Because of this, his brain had been "starved" of oxygen for a short while during birth. Some of his brain cells died. Miguel now suffered from a neurological disorder called cerebral palsy. Palsy refers to the spastic, jerky way by which he must move. In addition, like thirty percent of all people with cerebral palsy, Miguel was mentally retarded. Although Maria was four years younger, Miguel and she were in the same grade.

Miguel was a friendly, practical guy who was quite comfortable with his handicap. In fact, his major constructive criticism of well-intentioned strangers who pitied him needlessly was that they were handicapping the handicapped. With two crutches he was able to walk adequately. His school work was average at best. He realized early he probably would not become an eminent physicist or engineer like his parents; however he would endeavor to make his life worthy. He felt that all human beings had been born with some talent. All one had to do was find and develop it.

Miguel's interest was camping. He loved hiking, although his condition required that he be dependent on someone else for assistance. He enjoyed reading books on techniques of survival in the wilderness. His favorite novels were great westerns, like those of Louis L'Amour.

At school, when his deformed physique frightened kids, his wry sense of humor put them at ease. Only a few disliked him; but these few made his life difficult at times. One such person was the cool and calculating captain of the skating team, Tim Yacama. At the age of fourteen, Tim had already grown to a height of six feet. Well built and robust, Tim was one of the most talented and famous skaters of the region. Miguel loved to watch Tim skate. Even as Miguel cherished the calypso, salsa, and reggae dances of his West Indian culture, he was open and could appreciate the beauty of gracefully gliding Tim Yacama skating on the ice. Yet they were not the best of friends.

Often, on his way to school, Tim would manage to trip Miguel in the snow. Tim would say, "Miguel, I am so sorry you fell again."

With the help of his sister, Maria, Miguel got back to his feet. She also helped him to control his angry desires to cudgel Tim. They had been taught to be pacifists and to respond to violence with peace. Their parents were devoted supporters of Mahatma Gandhi and Dr. Martin Luther King. Fully embracing the philosophy of non-violence espoused by King, they advised their children not to quench their thirst for justice and freedom "by drinking from the cup of bitterness and hatred" (Martin Luther King). Yet it was times like these when he regretted his handicap the most, because the handicap restrained him from responding to his anger.

On the way home, Miguel and Maria happened to pass by a frozen pond where Tim was practicing. They were captivated by his grace. In his smugness, Tim performed for his newly -arrived audience. Preoccupied with his performance, Tim forgot to avoid the partially frozen part of the pond. As he emerged from doing a triplet, he found himself submerged in the pond. He tried to raise himself, but the icy edge broke in his hands with each attempt. Maria became terrified. With his camping knowledge, Miguel rose to the challenge and responded to Tim's frantic cries for help. Slipping and sliding, Maria and Miguel came within ten feet of Tim. To go closer would have been dangerous on such thin ice. With his crutches tied end to end by a scarf, Miguel advanced his makeshift pole to Tim while Maria anchored him by his feet:

When Tim caught the pole, Miguel hollered to Maria to pull with all her might. Miguel held tightly to the pole but his grasp was slipping. Just as the scarf tore, Tim was pulled to safety.

Tim had difficulty in thanking Miguel. Miguel realized how humiliated Tim felt and comforted him, "Forget the past, Tim. Let's be friends."

"But how can I make this up to you?"

"How about teaching me and Maria how to toboggan?"

"Sure, and I'll make certain you don't fall anymore on the way to school. I'll carry you in the toboggan."

"Sure bet!"

This is how a bully and a crippled child became the best of friends.

Win or Lose

The Todds were a family of three: father, mother, and son. The father was a tall, muscular fellow who was moderately obese. A few extra beers on many a weekend over several decades left him a large protuberance at his belt buckle. The mother was a slim, energetic woman who knew that on TV sports nights, her husband and son were not to be disturbed except for life and death matters. The son was a bright, active child who loved sports and liked to collect insects. He wanted to be an entomologist. Both father and son were avid basketball fans.

It was Friday night. The Boston Celtics were battling the Los Angeles Lakers for the championship. The game began. As their family tradition would have it, Mrs. Todd brought popcorn and Kool-Aid for her son and a dark imported beer for her husband.

The Celtics were leading for most of the game, leaving father and son in good spirits. The end approached. The Celtic's lead slipped. Father Todd shook his left fist at the TV in despair. His son shouted and screamed. The Celtics led only by one point. Both son and father moved to the edge of their seats. The Celtics trailed by one. In outrage, Father Todd shouted with fury.

Suddenly, he grabbed his chest and his left hand was clenched. His voice choked. Aware that something awful was happening as his father changed from a smile to a frown, the son called his mother. The Celtics had lost championships before but their dismal performance had never caused his father to develop beads of sweat on his forehead, pallor, or difficulty in breathing. "Oh, the pressure upon my chest," his father cried out. Father Todd began to vomit and fell to the floor, unconscious.

Mrs. Todd ran to his rescue. She checked his airway. Perhaps he gulped too much beer when Larry Bird missed a key shot. She found neither respiration nor pulse. While telling her son to call the ambulance, she began cardiopulmonary resuscitation.

As the ambulance sirens signaled the arrival of the paramedics, Father Todd returned to consciousness. Because of her first aid training, Mrs. Todd was able to prevent a fatal heart attack and save her husband's life.

After recovery, Father Todd was determined to minimize his risks of heart attack by exercising regularly, ceasing to smoke, losing excess weight—and feeling good about life whether the Celtics won or lost.

Tetralogy of Fallot

Bo Smith was a young man who was in the hospital because he had a very serious heart defect. Now that he was seventeen years of age, he was old enough to undergo an operation to fix the defect. Although Bo had been told by his parents that he had a bad heart, he had always wanted to ask the doctor exactly what was this defect that had kept him from playing football or running track but not from doing his homework. He wanted to understand why he had not grown as tall and robust as his brothers or why his heart had made the ends of his fingers look like clubs. He wondered why his body was different from others.

Later in the day, when the doctor entered his room, Bo gathered his confidence and asked, "Doctor, what is wrong with my heart? Why must I have this operation?"

"You have pink Tetralogy of Fallot," the doctor replied.

"But I'm not pink. My skin is dark coffee brown," exclaimed Bo.

"No," the doctor chuckled, "I did not mean to imply that you were pink. The word 'pink' means that you have a milder form of a congenital heart defect."

"What does Tetralogy of Fallot mean?" asked Bo.

"Tetralogy," replied the doctor, "means there are four related aspects of the problem. It is derived from the Greek words tetra and logy. 'Tetra' means four. 'Logy' means expression or study of. Thus, your heart expresses four related defects."

"Can you explain them to me please?" Bo asked.

"All right," said the doctor. "The heart has four chambers, or what you can call rooms. These rooms are connected.

"Normally, there are only openings or doors between an upper and lower room. Blood flows from the upper to the lower rooms. There should be no doors between the two upper rooms or the two lower roams. This means that blood cannot flow directly from the left lower room to the right lower room. Yet, in your heart, blood can flow directly between the two lower rooms because of an abnormal opening in the wall. This opening is called a ventricular septal defect, 'Ventricular' refers to the room. 'Septal' refers to the wall. This is the first defect of your heart. The second defect in your heart is that the right lower chamber is much larger than it should be. This is called right ventricular hypertrophy. 'Hypertrophy' means enlargement. Understand?"

31

"Yes. But where is the blood going once it gets to the lower chambers?" Bo asked.

"It leaves the right lower chamber by a vessel called the pulmonary artery," the doctor replied. "Blood leaves the left lower chamber by a vessel called the aorta. The third defect in your heart is that the aorta receives blood from both lower rooms instead of just one. The fourth defect is that the pulmonary artery is smaller than it should be. Because of these four defects, your heart does not pump blood very well. The operation will help your heart to pump blood better to the rest of your body.

"What will the surgeon do in the operation?" Bo asked.

"Most likely," the doctor replied, "they will make two corrections. First, they will put a patch over the opening between the two lower chambers. Second, they will widen the pulmonary artery. This operation has been done successfully many times before."

"But who is Fallot?" Bo asked.

"Dr. Etienne-Louis Arthur Fallot was a French doctor who lived from 1850 to 1911," replied the doctor. "He was very interested in anatomy. He was one of the first doctors to understand the four malformations involved in the type of congenital heart disease that you have."

"Thank you, Doctor, very much," said Bo. "Now that I understand better what is wrong with my heart, I can go through with the operation."

Men Can Be Nurses, Too!

There he was, imprisoned in a hospital on the Fourth of July, surrounded by toddlers with runny noses, girls with childish dolls, and babies who never stopped crying. Then, as the ultimate inconvenience, a female nurse came to give him a shot in the rear end and take his temperature, blood pressure, pulse, and breathing rate every three or four hours. Gary had always thought hospitals were fancy hotels. He never dreamed a hospital could be such a noisy environment. Good thing he only had three more days to go before his discharge from the hospital. At the age of nine, Gary had four aims in life: to catch frogs, play football, become a mathematician, and to avoid at all costs giggling girls.

To his surprise today, instead of his regular nurse, Cathy, a man had come to give the pain medication and take his vital signs. He was built not unlike Archie Griffin, his favorite football star.

"Sir, are you a doctor?" Gary asked, excited that a doctor had come to see him.

"Hi, Gary. I'm Frank, your nurse for today. Cathy has the Fourth of July off. I am substituting for her."

"I did not know men could be nurses. That's women's work."

"Gary, do I look like a woman? If so, I'll ask Dr. Thomas to have your eyes examined," Frank teased.

"Sorry. I just thought all nurses were women," Gary apologized.

"A nurse is a special kind of person who is trained to help keep you healthy and to care for you when sickness occurs. It's not the sex but rather the kind of person that determines whether one can be a nurse."

"What's the difference between a nurse and a doctor?" asked Gary.

"A nurse formulates a plan of care within the framework provided by the physician."

"In the beginning, though, weren't all nurses women? No offense, of course," cautiously Gary inquired.

"In the beginning, there were no professional nurses. A sick person was cared for at home by a mother, sister, daughter as supervised by the visiting country doctor. The only drugs were folk medicines. When hospitals developed, nursing was considered menial employment. Few skills or aptitude were needed. Appalled by the state of health care, Florence Nightingale, who lived from 1820 to 1910 reformed the profession and made it honorable. Today nurses must keep abreast of the latest drugs and know how to use the

33

newest devices such as heart defibrillators, transducers, and dialysis machines. There is a great demand for nurses. Unlike many other professions, there is always employment available and good pay. In most hospitals there are seventy nurses for every one hundred patients."

"What do you have to do to become a nurse?"

"As I said before, it's not the sex but rather if you possess good health, physical stamina, emotional stability, dependability, and desire to contribute to the welfare of humanity. Then one enrolls in a two, three, four, or five-year nursing school, depending on whether you want an associate degree, diploma, or baccalaureate degree. Upon graduation, nurses receive an official nursing school cap or chevron and pin. They take the Nightingale pledge, pledging themselves to serve others, to maintain highest standards of personal morals, to aid the physician, and to respect the confidences and privacy of every patient. To practice nursing one must pass the state exams and obtain a license."

"Are there lots of guys in your class?" asked Gary.

"Sure. Well, more than there used to be. More men are discovering nursing is an honorable profession with a good, steady income. I used to think if I played professional football, I would get rich quick and not have to learn any other skills. But one day I broke the bones and tore the ligaments of my right knee, just like you. The next year I was dropped from the team. I switched colleges and entered a nursing program. Best move I ever made. Look, Gary, I must go but I'll be back later."

After Frank left, Gary pondered, "That's interesting. Men can be nurses, too." For the first time since being in the hospital, Gary looked forward to his next shot. With male nurses like Frank around, it wasn't so bad being in the hospital after all.

Trevor Shillito

Trevor Shillito wanted to be the first human on Mars. At the very least, he would step foot on the moon someday. He planned to be an astronaut.

When he came of age, he enlisted in the Air Force. When all of the entrance exams and physical check-ups were finished, he expected no less than to be sent to officer school.

"Son," said the lieutenant, "I am sorry. We cannot accept you because your heart would not be able to withstand the rigorous training. Dr. Sezari will be here shortly to explain the reason more fully. Here he is now."

"Good morning, sir," said Trevor.

"Good morning, Mr. Shillito," said Dr. Sezari. Trevor, you have been disappointed by the news, I am sure. We were equally disappointed. You scored very well in all the other categories. The problem is your heart. You have a heart murmur. Did you ever have rheumatic fever?"

"Not that I know of. I can ask my parents about it," said Trevor.

"Well, that doesn't surprise me. Half of the people with rheumatic heart disease can't remember having had it."

"What is rheumatic fever and heart disease?"

"Rheumatic fever is a recurring febrile illness caused by the *Streptococcus* bacteria. It is characterized by a sore throat, subcutaneous nodules, abnormal movements called Sydenham's chorea, a rash called *erythema marginatum*, and heart disease. In the heart, the valves are particularly affected. The valves become rigid and thickened."

"I see. That's why there is a murmur. The flow of blood is interrupted by the abnormal valves, causing turbulence."

"Well, son, that's right. You are pretty good in engineering," eyed the doctor.

"Yes, sir."

"Perhaps there is a place for you in the aerospace field after all. Ever consider applying for a job as engineer down at Cape Canaveral?"

"No, sir, but I will look into the possibility."

"Trevor, I know you are interested in landing on planets, but truthfully, most anyone can do that given the right equipment, directions, and technology. What we need are more people who can provide the means for landing on planets. If you want a worthy mission in life, try that one on for size."

On the way home, Trevor Shillito was not discouraged. Maybe he wouldn't be the person to step foot on Mars first, but he sure would be on the team that would make it possible for that astronaut to do it.

Rabbits Are Not The Only Ones Who Need Rabbit Food

The Elmore High School tenth grade class had a new student this year. Her name was Carolyn Mae McKenzie. She had come from Newbern, North Carolina. Although she spoke differently from her northern raised classmates, she was a good student who always did her homework and, in general, enjoyed learning. After a month, it seemed she could almost like the North as much as the South.

One morning, strangely enough, she did not feel like going to school. Then she asked her mom about her malaise, her mother felt she probably had eaten too much "wrinkled steak" the night before. (Wrinkled steak is known as chitterlings or hog guts in the South.) After a breakfast of freshly juiced apples and hominy grits, Carolyn went off to school. She felt stronger but now she noticed there was pain around her navel. Although Carolyn's habit was to run to school in order to improve her track time, today she walked. Running made the pain worse. During biology class that morning they were supposed to dissect the frog. As Carolyn was interested in aquatic life, she had looked forward to this session. Yet after the first fifteen minutes, she became nauseated and then vomited. She was taken immediately to the school nurse, who thought she had either become queasy because she was not used to dissection or that she had gastroenteritis. In either case, she was dismissed from school for the day. At noontime, Carolyn's brother, Ron, escorted her home. In an effort to cheer her, he tickled her. Carolyn felt herself involuntarily recoil from him when he touched her on the right side. By the time they reached home, the lower right-sided pain had become acute. She was in tears.

In an effort to calm her daughter, Mrs. McKenzie brought out Carolyn's favorite dish—a sparkling, juicy, red, sweet Georgia ham. (Georgia ham is known as watermelon in the South.) Carolyn, to everyone's surprise, wanted no part of it. At this point, Mrs. McKenzie knew she was ill. Her mother's intuition told her this was no regular stomachache.

She took her temperature. Carolyn had a fever. It was time to call Dr. Wheelcox. After a telephone consultation with Dr. Wheelcox, Mrs. McKenzie took her to his office.

After an exam, Dr. Wheelcox felt Carolyn had appendicitis and needed to be admitted to the hospital. Carolyn needed to have an appendectomy. He explained to them that the appendix is a vestigial, meaning no longer used, part of the intestines.

Hers had become inflamed. If it ruptured, then Carolyn would develop a raging infection in the form of peritonitis and possibly die. In girls, it is especially important to prevent the appendix from rupturing because peritonitis can harm the ovaries, thus making her sterile. Appendicitis can be caused by obstruction of the appendix secondary to
hardened pieces of stool, excessive local growth, foreign bodies, or parasites.

After contacting Mr. McKenzie, they decided to perform the operation. It was a success. Carolyn had pain afterwards but it was not half as intense as it was before the operation. On the sixth post-operative day, Carolyn was to come home. Before they left the hospital, Dr. Wheelcox gave Carolyn important advice. In the appendix, a hardened piece of stool was found. He warned her that other bowel problems might occur later in life if she did not improve her diet now. From now on, she would have to eat more vegetables.

In celebration, her mother cooked her favorite dinner with a new addition, according to doctor's orders: rabbit food, hoe cake, hoppin' John, and trotters. Mm! Mm! Good! (In the South, rabbit food is known as salad, hoe cake is fried bread, hoppin' John is peas and rice, and trotters are pig feet.)

Running Deer

At fourteen years, she could run as swiftly as a deer on the plains, river-ride an appaloosa bareback, track rabbits in the forest, and teach the elders how to read and write English. She was Running Deer Joanna Montgomery, who lived on a Native American reservation in northwestern Oklahoma.

At fifteen years, Running Deer noticed she could no longer run as swiftly and she was easily tired. The only thing different in her life was that she had begun to menstruate six months ago. She decided to see the doctor.

"Dr. Yurby, I am easily fatigued. My grandmother says I am less vibrant than I was six moons ago. That is curious because I also started menstruating six months ago," stated Running Deer.

"Running Deer, do you have a heavy flow of blood during your periods?" asked Dr. Yurby.

"Yes."

After more questions about her history, especially her eating habits, Dr. Yurby conducted a physical exam and withdrew some blood from her arm for tests.

"Running Deer, the evidence thus far shows you probably have an iron deficiency anemia. Under the microscope your red blood cells look differently from the normal kind.

"Your cells are smaller and more pale than normal. As you have probably studied in school, iron is contained in the red blood cell. Thus if you lose blood then you also lose iron. When the iron supply is low in the body, then red blood cells are not made as well."

"You mean they become pale and small?" Running Deer clarified.

"Yes. You are correct," affirmed Dr. Yurby.
"Are there other causes of iron deficiency anemia?"

"Yes. As we discussed before, the number one cause is chronic blood loss. Two other causes are an iron deficient diet and an inherent defect in iron assimilation into the body."

"Dr. Yurby, is it normal for me to acquire this anemia?"

"Well, it is never normal to be anemic but iron deficiency anemia is common among young menstruating women. Ten to twenty percent of you are iron deficient as compared to less than five percent of men."

"Dr. Yurby, if iron is the fourth most abundant element in the soil of this area, why didn't my body just absorb more iron from the food when its supply became low?"

"Good question. Iron exists in more than one form and furthermore, different foods contain different levels of iron. Unless you eat the right combination of food, then you will have an inadequate intake of iron. The best sources of iron are liver, heart, brewer's yeast, spinach, wheat germ, eggs, oysters, some dried beans and fruit. Foods with very little iron are unfortified milk and non-green vegetables. A vitamin that enhances the body's uptake of iron is vitamin C. In general, meat is a moderate source of iron. To correct the anemia, we usually give iron pills."

"Thanks, Dr. Yurby. First I will try to improve my diet by eating foods high in iron, like liver and wheat germ. If I don't feel better in a month, I'll come back for the pills. It is best to work with nature first before taking the pills to do her job. Our tradition is to support before supplanting nature."

One month later, Running Deer could be seen running, riding, tracking, and teaching with a renewed vigor, determination, and natural glow of health.

The Best Form of Health Insurance

At the age of sixteen, Gustav showed potential to be a premiere violinist. He had been playing for nine years and yet it seemed as if there was never enough time devoted to his practice. The hours seemed as moments. The price of dedication was high, but the beauty of the music he created was priceless. He sought to bring each concerto, sonata, or song to life with a spirit of its own. Playing the violin, he often reflected, was like giving birth.

During one severe winter, Gustav became very weak with fever and chills. When he did not even feel like playing the violin, his family knew he was dangerously ill. His neck became stiff and rigid. His head ached while his vision dimmed. After several seizures, his family took him with great haste to Children's Hospital. A lab test showed his white blood cell count to be 17,000 (normal is 5000-10,000). White blood cells are the soldiers of the body. Whenever there is a battle raging in the body, they increase in number. By withdrawing some fluid from his spinal canal (a procedure which is called a lumbar puncture), the doctors discovered he had bacterial meningitis. Meningitis is an infection of the covering of the brain. Gustav was taken to the intensive care unit and begun on several drugs, including antibiotics, immediately. To get the medicine into his blood as quickly as possible, a small catheter was placed in a vein in his arm.

Through the night, his fever worsened. When he became stuporous, an emergency CAT scan was done. A CAT scan is a complex x-ray which produces an image of a person's internal anatomy. 'CAT' stands for computer automated tomography. The scan showed brain swelling and a small collection of fluid on the left side which was pushing the brain to the right side.

After much consultation, the neurosurgeon told Gustav's family that to save his brain, they would have to drill a small hole in his skull directly above the fluid collection. By expressing the fluid in this manner, the brain would be partially decompressed. With less pus on the brain's surface, antibiotics would be able to work better. His family consented.

By four days after the operation, Gustav had improved so well he was asking for his violin. After eighteen days, he had improved enough to go home.

Eighteen days away from his violin. What punishment! When he strummed his violin, he found his fingers had not forgotten their places on the fingerboard, nor had his hand forgotten how gently to hold the rosin-rubbed bow. His main disappointment was that his arms, like the rest of his body, were weak.

Gustav was determined never to be forced to leave his violin again. In order to do that, he knew it was necessary to stay healthy through exercise. Although to swim for one hour a day took time away from violin practice, Gustav was satisfied. Exercise, he figured, was one of the best forms of health insurance. By "paying" the premium of exercise, he bought protection for his health. He also found swimming strengthened his arms, cleared his mind, and added vigor to his general well-being. *Too bad,* he thought, *that we human beings must often suffer a serious illness before we learn the proper way to take care of our bodies.*

A Doctor in the Hills

Della's great-grandmother was at least 110 years old. She had been born in the hills of West Virginia and seemed as old and wise as the Appalachian mountains. Being with Granny was like reading an ancient history book. She could recount the history of Della's parents, grandparents, and great-great-grand parents. Her great-great-grandfather was a Choctaw Indian. Her great-great-grandmother was a slave who could haul her weight in cotton. Shortly after the Emancipation Proclamation was issued, Granny's parents moved from Montgomery, Alabama, to Wheeling, West Virginia. Granny was born three days after they arrived. Granny had some schooling but at the age of sixteen, she married Della's great-grandfather, the town blacksmith. They had ten children, but five died when a tuberculosis epidemic spread like wildfire in the hills one winter. Granny also became afflicted with the disease and felt her health had not been the same since.

This fact concerned Della very much. She didn't know much about tuberculosis but she understood that the quality of Granny's life could be improved if she had proper medical care. After much argument, Della convinced the family to call the doctor. Della called several doctors in the valley and finally found one who made house calls up in the hills. His name was Dr. Beddle.

After getting the history from them and doing a physical exam, Dr. Beddle spread some of Granny's urine and sputum on microscopic slides. By pricking her finger he withdrew some of her blood into a very small tube called a capillary tube. Using several machines in his medical van, he was able to collect laboratory results. Dr. Beddle called the family together.

"I have news for you. Mrs. Washington, when you stated that since you had tuberculosis, your health has not been the same, you were very correct. By looking at your sputum, I can still see *Mycobacterium tuberculosis*, which is the bacteria that causes tuberculosis. Consequently, I suspect the whole family has been exposed to tuberculosis and will have to be treated. All of you should come to the clinic tomorrow for special tests, shots, and medicine. We use antibiotics to fight the infection Before antibiotics, 200 people for every 100,000 Americans died of tuberculosis. Today, about four people for every 100,000 Americans die of tuberculosis. In the world today, about five million people die of tuberculosis every year. For blacks, Eskimos, and native Americans, it is especially important for them to be tested for tuberculosis because they have less natural immunity and thus are more susceptible to the disease. Understand? Questions?"

42

"How long must one take the antibiotics if one of us is found to be infected?" asked Della.

"One year."

"Well, Doc, thanks. That explains why that epidemic earlier this century killed more people up in these hills than down in the valley, where more whites live. Mighty grateful, Doc. See you in the morning," said Granny.

Della's family was proud of her and urged her to study medicine, since she seemed interested. Granny especially urged her to pursue medicine because she felt each generation should be able to do better and bigger things than the one which preceded it. Thus inspired, Della studied biology, chemistry, physics, math, and English in school. She attended West Virginia State University and majored in biochemistry, then continued to study medicine at the medical school. After four years of college, four years of medical school, and three years of a medical residency at the Charleston Area Medical Center, Della came back home to be the first doctor in her family and community. She served the people of the hills well.

Crying Wolf

John and Jamie Whittaker were fraternal twins. "Fraternal" refers to the fact that they were born at the same time but do not look alike. Because each one developed from his own separate egg, they were not identical. Identical twins develop from the same egg.

When John was seventeen years old, his vision worsened. After seeing the eye doctor, an ophthalmologist, he received a pair of brown horn-rimmed glasses. The next day, Jamie remarked at dinner that his vision was dimming, too.

"Jamie Whittaker, when will you grow out of that childish habit of yours in which you always want what John wants?" scolded his mother. "If your vision was worsening, why didn't you mention it when I was making an appointment for John last month?"

"Now Beatrice," calmed Mr. Whittaker, "simmer down. Jamie, in the past, you have cried wolf on numerous occasions. Remember the time John got a bad ear infection and needed his hearing checked. The next day, you also claimed deafness. We checked your hearing and it was perfect. Remember the time John had palpitations and needed his heart checked by the cardiologist. The next day, you claimed to have chest pain. We spent much money to check your heart function and found no supporting evidence for abnormality. There are many other episodes of this nature in the past. You are seventeen now. It's time you took a call for help seriously. Crying wolf is a dangerous and possibly fatal habit. Now, do you really have a change in vision?"

"Yes, Mom and Dad," earnestly replied Jamie.

"All right, Beatrice, take him back to Dr. Spencer," ordered Mr. Whittaker.

After examining Jamie, Dr. Spencer called Mrs. Whittaker into his office.

"Beatrice, Jamie is not joking this time. He has a vision change but he also has headaches and some other signs that concern me. I need to do further tests."

"Okay. What else needs to be done?"

"I would like to get a brain CAT scan, which is a fancy and sophisticated x-ray, next week."

The Whittakers returned to the office after the studies were completed.

"Jamie, we have done some tests as you know. Based on the results, I think you have been having visual changes and headaches because of a growth in a particular region of the brain. This region is close to the optic tract. I think you have a kind of brain tumor called craniopharyngioma."

"Dr. Spencer," asked Mr. Whittaker, "can it be cured? "Will he live?"

"Yes, there is a possibility it can be cured by surgery. We can make a 'window' in the skull, which will allow us to approach the tumor and excise it. Although his vision may still be decreased, he has a good chance to survive."

After more consultation, the Whittakers consented to the surgery. While he was recovering from the operation, Jamie had much time for reflection about his habit of crying wolf. This illness showed him how dangerous it was to fake sickness for attention. From now on, he would find more constructive ways to distinguish himself. Life would be more rewarding if instead of provoking his mother's anger by faking sickness, he could win his mother's affection by performing better in school. One year later, Jamie was graduated valedictorian from his high school.

Who's Counting

Jill Dilsey had a crush on Ted Nelson. She loved the ground he walked on and the air he breathed. When she was placed in his classroom, her parents found that their truant daughter, who was known for skipping classes, was now bringing home report cards with 100 percent attendance rates. The splendor of love was upon them. Her parents were grateful because this was the first time they had seen their daughter happy since her brother, Carlyle, died in a drunk driving accident one year ago.

On Friday, Jill and Ted went to a basketball game and then to a party for seniors only. There was much alcohol there but it made Jill shudder just to look at it. It reminded her of how Carlyle's excessive alcohol intake made him waste his potential and destroy his life before he reached the age of twenty.

"Have a beer," offered Ted.

"No, thank you, and I don't think you should have another one either," answered Jill curtly.

"Who's counting? Certainly not me."

"Ted, you are going to end up like Carlyle soon!"

"Look, Jill. I've only had two beers. Let's sit down and talk about this," comforted Ted. Tears were already welling up in her eyes.

"It all started in high school. Carlyle would come home from school and go straight for Dad's bar where the whiskey was kept. By the time be was a senior, he spent more time being intoxicated than sober. Then his liver began to fail; he became yellow and his feet became swollen. Because of the way he preferred to drink alcohol rather than eat a decent meal, he stayed sick. Whenever he talked, he would tell long insensible stories. His memory, which was once the best in the class, deteriorated and he failed several courses. After a party one night, he left almost stuporous but refused to let anyone drive him home. Two hours later he was found dead after driving off a bridge."

The grief Jill thought was gone came back full force. Ted took her hand and held her closely.

"Look, Jill. You've been through a lot. Let's go."

Jill was glad to leave the raucous party. A cool night zephyr refreshed them as they walked home. Jill was sad but Ted knew how to make her happy.

"Jill, will you marry me?" asked Ted.

She smiled. "Only on two conditions. That you love me, that's number one. Number two is that there be no alcohol in our house."

"But Jill, everyone drinks alcohol!" Ted protested.

"Not in our house," Jill retorted.

"Okay, okay. How about wine at dinner? Wouldn't that be romantic, honey?" Ted suggested.

"Well, since marriage means giving and taking, I'll compromise. Wine only on special occasions." They both laughed in their happiness.

One year later, they were married. When they reached their fifth anniversary, Ted could still count the number of beers he had bought since that night he had become engaged to his beloved wife Jill.

A Quest for the Key to the Lock

Garland Alexander was at the peak of his glory. This senior year at Jefferson High School, he was captain of the weight lifting team and president of his class. He had been accepted into Oregon's best colleges. He wanted to be a politician because he was dedicated to the welfare and future of the state. Little did he know then that six months later he would decide instead to spend the rest of his life in a laboratory working against time on a problem as crucial as life itself.

While lifting weights one day, Garland noticed a large bulge in his groin area. When he called his doctor about it, she said it may be a hernia but Garland should come in for an examination to make sure all else was well.

After some questions about his general state of health, Dr. Chung found that Garland had also been having night sweats, itching, fevers off and on, sore throat, and headaches. On physical exam, Dr. Chung found he had lost twenty pounds from last year. In addition to the hernia, she found his spleen to be enlarged and several large, matted, firm, non-tender lymph nodes in the neck region.

"Garland, you have a hernia, as we suspected. Yet these other findings raise the index of suspicion for another disease. I suspect you may have Hodgkin's disease or, less likely, infectious mononucleosis. I need to do further tests to be sure."

"Dr. Chung, I can't believe it. I am at the peak of my glory. What is Hodgkin's disease?"

"Hodgkin's is a malignant tumor of the lymph nodes and spleen. Its cause is unknown but is related to a weakness in the individual's immune system."

"How many people acquire it?"

"Three per 100,000 Americans acquire it every year. In general, you have an eighty percent chance of living in five years, if you have chemotherapy and radiation treatment."

"How come someone has not discovered a cure yet, Dr. Chung?"

"Cures are the result of scientific research. With the government cutbacks lately, there are less funds available to do research. Private funds are more and more the main support for research."

"What does a scientist do when he conducts research, Dr. Chung?"

"Did you ever read *Arrowsmith* by Sinclair Lewis in school?"

"No."

"In this book, Lewis characterizes Dr. Gottlieb, the research scientist, as the following: 'He wanted to look behind details and impressive-sounding lists of technical terms for the causes of things, for general rules which might reduce the chaos of dissimilar and contradictory symptoms to the orderliness of chemistry.' Doing research, Garland, is the one way we can change the course of humanity for the better. Finding cures through systematic research saves lives and improves the quality of those living. Finding the key to the lock of disease opens the door to progress."

When Garland left the office he was resolved to do research on Hodgkin's disease. Instead of politics, he would pursue a career in medical science. He went to college for four years, majoring in chemistry and graduating with honors. He went to medical school for four years to obtain an M.D. For two more years he studied in the laboratory of an oncologist to obtain his Ph.D. He completed a three-year residency in medicine. Thus well-educated in knowledge and technique, he became a professor and established his own laboratory dedicated to the study of Hodgkin's disease.

The Grass Is Greener in Your Own Backyard

"No, Beri, you can't skip breakfast to go horseback riding because you'll get low blood sugar from your morning insulin injection," Mrs. Smith informed her daughter who was already dressed in her equestrian attire.

"All right, if I have to eat breakfast, then I want waffles with blueberries, butter, and syrup," Beri demanded.

"No. Don't be silly, young lady. It's not on the diabetic diet list of acceptable breakfast items. You will get high blood sugar if I allow you to do that," firmly stated Mrs. Smith.

"That's the point, Mom. I am not a child anymore. I am grown. This is my body and my life," Beri screamed as she ran up the stairs to her room. Only one year, she thought, until graduation and freedom. Meanwhile she would fix her mom.

For the next week, Beri broke all the rules about diet and hygiene she had learned when she was first diagnosed as having diabetes ten years ago. She skipped her insulin injections. She ate whatever and whenever she pleased. She never tested her blood for sugar. A few days later when Mrs. Smith came to wake her for school, Beri did not respond. When she came the second time to wake her, Beri was having seizures. Her parents rushed her to the hospital.

The doctors found she was in diabetic coma. After a few days of intensive therapy, she awakened to find that she was in the hospital. Within reach there was another girl.

"Hi, I'm Beri Smith. What's your name?"

"Hi. I'm Coe Tillson. You've been asleep a long time. How are you?"

"Fine, I guess. Why are you here?"

"I was in a fire. My legs were burned very badly."

"Coe, how did it happen?"

"Faulty wiring in our house caused it."

"Is everyone else all right? Where's your family?" asked Beri cautiously.

"I am the only one who escaped. The rest of my family is dead."

"I am sorry to hear that, Coe. How do you feel?"

"Awful. I especially miss my mother. You don't realize how much you need someone until he or she is gone....Here comes your doctor, Beri."

"Hello, young lady!" welcomed Dr. Poulos. "I see you've met your roommate. How are you?"

"Okay. What happened?"

"Your blood sugar level went extremely high. You went into diabetic ketoacidosis. You were brought to the hospital when your mom found you to be in a coma and having seizures. She saved your life."

"Yes, we have been through this before, haven't we, Dr. Poulos?"

"Yes and," Dr. Poulos added, "each time you recover, I explain that in this form of retaliation against your mother, you only hurt yourself more. Do you know what the complications of diabetes are?"

"No," said Beri, because she didn't feel like talking.

"Do you, Coe?"

"Sure. Isn't blindness one?"

"Yes. Diabetes is the second leading cause of blindness in our country. Other complications are increased susceptibility to infection, gallstones, arteriosclerosis, skin ulcers, and gangrene of the extremities, among many others."

"Who discovered insulin, Dr. Poulos?" asked Beri, taking a sudden interest in conversation.

"We give credit for the discovery of insulin to Banting and Best in 1921. The first human being to receive insulin was an adolescent named Leonard Thompson, who came to the Toronto General Hospital in the same state you were in a few days ago. After several insulin injections, they noted '…the boy became brighter, looked better and said he felt stronger'."

"Well, Dr. Poulos, I do feel better."

"Good. I'll be back later to check on you."

"Beri, I used to be bitter about my mom, too, until I lost her. Now I miss her very much, even if she did nag a lot."

"Sure, Coe, I think I know what you mean. Just think, if I had lived in 1920, I would have died behaving the way I did last week. I am lucky to be alive."

"Try opening up to your mom. Try not to respond to her with bitterness or anger. You'll regret it later, like I do. Sometimes when mothers nag, you wish for another one. You think the grass is greener on the other side, but it's not true."

"Yes. You're night, Coe. The grass is greener in your own backyard."

A New Companion

With great anticipation, Sam Woodward looked forward to the arrival of his new brother or sister. His mom was six months pregnant. Sam had waited ten years for this event. As an only child, he discovered he received much personal attention from his parents but there were times when they were not interested in climbing trees, catching frogs, or building sandcastles. Sam desired a new companion.

When Mrs. Woodward was seven months pregnant, her abdomen became very large. His dad took her to the hospital for a few days.

"Why did Mom go, Dad?" asked Sam.

"There was too much fluid surrounding the baby. In the hospital, the doctors are removing some of the fluid from the bag of waters surrounding the baby."

"Dad, where did the fluid come from?"

"Son, the bag of waters surrounds the baby until he is born. This bag is called the amniotic sac. The fluid is called amniotic fluid. Easy, right? Now when you urinate, fluid flows out of the kidneys and into the toilet. When the baby urinates, he excretes the urine into this bag of waters. This bag of waters must remain at a certain level, meaning there must not be too little or too much fluid in it. As the baby urinates into the bag, fluid leaves the bag by two ways. In the first way, fluid is reabsorbed by Mom. In the second way, fluid goes back into the baby, meaning he swallows it."

"Oh yuck, the baby drinks urine?" asked Sam incredulously.

"Yes, that sounds unpleasant and I don't recommend you try it. However, you should understand that urine is sterile until it comes in contact with the outside environment."

"Dad, how come the bag became filled with too much water?"

"Sam, when there is too much fluid in the bag of waters, this state is called polyhydramnios. 'Poly' stands for many or much. 'Hydr' stands for water. 'Amnios' stands for the amniotic sac or the bag. When polyhydramnios exists, that means either too much urine is entering or not enough fluid is leaving by the two routes we talked about earlier. Understand?"

"I see."

When Sam's mom had four weeks to go before the estimated date of delivery, she entered premature labor and gave birth to Ethan Woodward, Sam's new brother. Soon after his birth, the doctors discovered that Ethan had a block in his digestive tract. The doctor explained it to the Woodward family.

"Ethan's doing well, except for a small problem he has in swallowing. Normally, food and drink pass from the mouth, down the food tube, which is the esophagus, and then into the stomach. Ethan has a narrowed food tube. The name of this congenital birth defect is called esophageal atresia. Atresia means narrowing."

"Dr. Orbyle, how can this be fixed?" Mr. Woodward inquired.

"It is easily fixed by doing an operation. In the operation, we will widen the narrowed esophagus. While the esophagus is healing, we will feed him by another route—a manmade route which connects the stomach to the outside environment.

"In this manner, we can feed him through the gastrostomy tube until the esophagus heals."

"Thanks, Dr. Orbyle," replied everyone.

A few weeks later, Ethan had his tube removed and was strong enough to come home. Sam took extra care in feeding his brother. He wanted to make sure Ethan would be strong enough a companion to climb trees, catch frogs, and build sandcastles.

A Citation from the President

During the summers they stayed in Mobile, Alabama, Alistair Gambol spent more time sailing and swimming in the Gulf of Mexico than he did on land. To sail the clear blue gulf on an even keel was truly one of life's greatest pleasures.

While sailing was a pleasure to Alistair, he also knew it could be a dangerous sport if the proper precautions were not taken. Alistair took cardiopulmonary resuscitation, first aid and water safety courses every year in order to learn the latest techniques and regulations. He took the sailing sport seriously and always wore a safety jacket. To do less was to ask for trouble.

On one particular halcyon day while sailing, Alistair saw his neighbors water skiing without life jackets. Smiling, they waved to him. Then Alistair noticed that not only did they lack life jackets but also only one person was driving the boat. According to regulations, there should be two people—one to drive and one to watch the person who was skiing.

Suddenly and without a sound, Marilyn slipped into the water. Her husband Jim did not notice and kept driving ahead in the boat. Alarmed, Alistair deftly turned his boat to go in her direction. He saw her surface briefly once and then disappear again. As he came within ten meters of the spot where she had originally fallen, she surfaced again fifteen meters slightly to the left. Alistair quickly tacked his boat toward the left while throwing out a long rope. Alistair became afraid that the undercurrent of the gulf was going to drown her. In the distance he heard Jim shouting frantically, "Marilyn! Help Marilyn!"

Just then, he felt a weak tug on the rope. In response, he began to tow the line in. Marilyn surfaced. With great difficulty, Alistair pulled her limp body to the boat. She was still conscious but very frightened. She felt nauseated because she had gulped much sea water while flailing to stay afloat.

"Marilyn, are you all right? You nearly drowned because you didn't have a life jacket," said Alistair.

Jim brought his speedboat alongside the sailboat.

"Thanks, Alistair, for saving her life. Are you all right, Marilyn?" Jim anxiously asked.

"Yes, except I feel weak," she replied.

They took her to the hospital immediately, where she remained for a few days to recover. Afterwards, Jim said, "Alistair, we sure are grateful. How can I ever repay you?"

"Well, if you're serious about that, then you can repay me by taking water safety classes and obeying the water skiing regulations. The next time you may not be so lucky," warned Alistair.

"You're right, Alistair. We will register today to take the courses."

For the service he rendered in the saving of Marilyn Tyke's life, Alistair Gambol received a citation of honor from the President of the United States of America.

A Sharp Shooter

Fay Refsum had eyes as sharp as an eagle's. She was the top sharp shoot-er in her police academy class, which consisted of forty men and six women.

When the final practical exam was six months away, Fay developed a nervous tremor she could not control. Whereas before her iron will could prevent her heart from racing in the most terrifying of circumstances, now she had palpitations even while sleeping. Her uniform fitted loosely because of weight loss, although her appetite was voracious. On the coldest of days, she walked to class without a coat. When her brother came for a visit, he noticed she had developed a stare.

"Why don't you see the doctor, sis?" advised her brother.

"You are right. Why, last week during shooting practice I missed the tar-get completely. Everybody thinks I am losing my nerve, but it seems to me, I am more nervous than ever. I'll see the doctor in the morning."

After the physical exam, Dr. Hall called her into his office.

"Fay, I think you have a thyroid disease called Grave's disease. Have you ever noticed how full the lower part of your neck has become?"

"Not really, sir," she said, feeling her neck. There was a swelling at the base of her neck, right below the Adam's apple.

"Fay, you have hyperthyroidism. That means your thyroid gland is pro-ducing too much thyroid hormone. The excess thyroid hormone is giving you these symptoms and signs. After we treat you, these will go away and you'll feel like your regular self again."

After talking with him further, Fay consented to taking the medicine. Five months later, she was top scorer again on all the exams, especially the target shooting section.

O Lord Jesus Christ
(derived from Psalm 51)

O Lord Jesus Christ, Son of God
Have mercy upon me
According to thy loving kindness
And all thy tender mercy

Wash me from my iniquity
Cleanse me from my sin
Purge me with thy hyssop pure
And I shall be made clean

Make me to hear thy joy again
Thy gladness in my bones
Hide thy face from my sins
Blot out mine iniquities

Create in me a clean heart
O God renew in me
The joy of thy salvation
Uphold me with thine hand

O Lord open thou my lips for thee
My mouth shall shew forth thy praise
For thou desirest a contrite heart
Thou art pleased with righteousness

Blessed Beatitudes
(Matthew 5)

Blessed be the Lord
With righteousness He rules
His kingdom reigns

Blessed are the poor in spirit
For theirs is the kingdom of heaven
Blessed are the pure in heart
For they shall see God

Blessed are they which do hunger and thirst after righteousness
For they shall be filled
Blessed are the meek for they shall inherit the earth

Blessed are they which are persecuted for righteousness
For theirs is the kingdom of heaven
Blessed are they that mourn for they shall be comforted

Blessed are the peacemakers
For they shall be called the children of God
Blessed are the merciful for they shall obtain mercy

Bless
(Psalm 103)

Bless the Lord, O my soul and all that is within me
Bless His name, His holy name
Bless the Lord, O my soul

Forget not all His benefits
Who forgives all your iniquities
Who heals all your diseases
Who redeems your life from destruction

Who crowns you with love, with loving kindness and tender mercies
Who satisfies your mouth with good things
So that your youth is renewed like the eagle's

The Lord executes
Righteousness
And justice for all who are oppressed

He made known His ways to Moses
His acts to the children of Israel
The Lord is merciful and gracious

Slow to anger, abounding in mercy
He will not always strive with us
Nor will He keep His anger forever

He has not dealt with us, according to our sins
Nor punished us according to,
Our iniquities

For as the heavens are high above the earth
So great is His mercy
Toward those who fear Him

As far as the east from the west, so far has He removed our
Transgressions
As a father pities his kids

The Lord pities those who fear Him

For He knows our frame
He remembers that we are dust
As for man, as for man, His days are like the grass

As a flower of the field, so He flourishes
For the wind passes over it
And it is gone

And its place remembers it no more, but the mercy of the Lord
Is from everlasting to everlasting
On those who fear Him

And His righteousness to children's children
To such as keep His covenant
And do His commandments, the Lord has established His throne
His kingdom over all

Bless the Lord, all His angels excel in strength and do His word
Heeding the voice of His word
Bless the Lord all you hosts

You ministers of His who do His pleasure
Bless the Lord, all His works
In His dominion

Bless the Lord, all His angels excel in strength and do His word
Heeding the voice of His word
Bless the Lord, O my soul

Foxes Have Holes

He was born in a manger bed
He gave communion in a loaned room
He lay buried in a borrowed, a borrowed tomb

Foxes have holes
the sheep have their folds
but nowhere for the King with riches untold
lions have their den
bears have their cave
but nowhere for the Savior, His life He gave

The cattle have their drove
the wolves have their pack
but nowhere for the Savior, who fills our lack
the fish have their school
the birds have their nest
but nowhere for the Savior, His head to rest

I Believe in Miracles

I believe in miracles
they're a sign from God above
they show His power and His love
yes I believe in Him

I believe in miracles
they're a sign mysterious in kind
they show Christ's nature truly divine
yes I believe in Him

I believe in miracles
Christ had power over sin, disease, and death
He brought hope to the bereft
yes I believe in Him

I believe in miracles
Christ controls the universe
He dissolved death's sting and curse
yes I believe in Him

I believe in miracles
He healed the deaf and raised the dead
He gave Himself to be our bread
yes I believe in Him

Come on Board the Gospel Train

Come on board the gospel train
come on board both rich and poor
come on board, the bridegroom is coming
come on board before He shuts the door

Come on board, the bridegroom is coming
shed your sins and find your oil
let your light shine and be ye ready
take your place on the train royal

Come on board, the bridegroom is coming
the hour eleven will soon be here
the ticket is free but don't look back
the pay is the same, so do not fear

Come on board, the bridegroom is coming
here He awaits for your return
take a seat and He'll carry you
home at last, no more war to learn

The Doctor of My Soul

In the hem of His robe
is more healing
than all the world can know

In the cuff of His sleeve
there's more power and might
He's the doctor of my soul

With His finger of love, He can touch your heart
more then all the world can show

With the breath of His voice, He can still the wind
He's the doctor of my soul

In the laces of His shoes
is more worthiness
than all the world can hold

in the collar of His garment
there's more mercy and grace
He's the doctor of my soul

The Books of the Holy Bible

Genesis, Exodus, Leviticus, Numbers
Deuteronomy, Joshua
Judges, Ruth, Samuel, and Kings
Chronicles, Ezra, Nehemiah
Esther, Job, Psalms, Proverbs
Ecclesiastes, Song of Solomon
Isaiah, Jeremiah, Lamentations, Ezekial

Daniel, Hosea, Joel, Amos, Obadiah
Jonah, Micah, Nahum
Habakkuk, Zephaniah
Haggai
Zechariah and Malachi
Matthew, Mark, Luke, and John, Acts
Romans, Corinthians, Galatians, Ephesians

Philippians, Colossians
Thessalonians
Timothy, Titus, Philemon
Hebrews, James, Peter, and John
Jude, Revelation
These are the books of the Holy Bible

Prophecies

Prophecies of Christ's victories, give us blessed assurety

Isaiah told of birth from a virgin
Hosea told of the flight to Egypt
Jeremiah told of the holy innocents
Malachi told of the forerunner

David told of the Son of God
Isaiah told of His gentle ministry
Moses told of the prophet of prophets
Isaiah told a man of sorrows He would be

David told of a friend's betrayal
Zechariah told of a donkey riding king
David told of Melchizedek
Zechariah told of thirty coins pricing

Isaiah told of the death with inmates
Zechariah told of piercing the side and feet
David told of laughing scorn
David told of vinegar to eat

David told of parted garment
David told of unbroken bones
David told of Christ's resurrection
David told of Christ's ascension

Isaiah told it...Hosea told it...Jeremiah told it...Malachi told it,

Is Your Life a Mess or a Message

Is your life a mess or a message
His name do bless
don't straddle spiritual hedges
your side express

Pressed down, shaken, running over
give and it shall be given unto you.

Good measure in your bosom
will make you new
give and it shall be given
unto you

Cast your bread upon the water
praise His name
claim God as your only father
He stays the same

My Help Come from the Lord
(Psalm 121)

I will lift up mine eyes
unto the hills
from whence cometh
my help
my help cometh from
the Lord
who made heaven and earth

He will not suffer
thy foot to be removed
He who keeps you will not
slumber
behold He who keeps
Israel
shall not slumber
nor sleep

The Lord is your keeper
the Lord is your shade
at your right hand
the sun shall not strike you
by day
nor the moon by night

The Lord shall preserve
you from all evil
He shall preserve
your soul
the Lord shall preserve
your going and coming
from this time and evermore

Jesus Christ, the Light of Light

Mighty as an ocean wave
Deep as still waters
Strong as each man's passionate desire
Jesus Christ, the holy fire

Solemn as the snow in winter
purifying as the heat in summer
dazzling as the blossoms in spring
Jesus Christ, the king of kings

Glorious as the sun arising
noble as the setting sun
meek as the moon at midnight
Jesus Christ, the light of light

O Lord Our Lord
(Psalm 8)

O Lord our Lord
how excellent is your name
in all the earth
who has set your glory
above the heavens

Out of the mouth of babes
you have ordained strength
because of your enemies
that you may silence the enemy

When I consider your heavens
the work of your fingers
the moon and the stars
which you have ordained
what is man that you are mindful of him

And the Son of man
that you visit him
you have made him
a little lower than angels

You've crowned him with glory, honor
you've made him to have dominion
over the works of your hands
you have put all things under his feet
sheep and oxen, the beasts of the field

The birds of the air
the fish of the sea
that pass through the paths
of the seas

O Lord our Lord
how excellent is your name
in all the earth
who has set your glory
above the heavens.

Mary Had a Little Lamb

Mary had a little lamb, little lamb, little lamb
Mary had a little lamb, she called him Jesus

He fed 5000 souls one day, souls one day, souls one day
He fed 5000 souls one day, He knew the power of prayer

He taught about the golden rule, golden rule, golden rule
He taught about the golden rule, He knew the holy word

He changed the water into wine, into wine, into wine
He changed the water into wine, He is the bridegroom

He gave sight to the blind, to the blind, to the blind
He gave sight to the blind, physician to my soul

He stilled the waters with his word, with his word, with his word
He stilled the waters with His word, all honor to His name

Crucified, He died for me, died for me, died for me
Crucified, He died for me, precious is His name

On Easter day, He rose again, rose again, rose again
on Easter day, He rose again, all glory to His name

Mary had a little lamb, little lamb, little lamb
Mary had a little lamb, she called him Jesus.

Saints

I want to be in that number when the saints come marching in
Oh when the saints come marching in

O when that saint whom we call Paul
he fully answered Christ's call

O when that saint whom we call Jude
he left a letter of how God viewed

O when that saint whom we call John
he wrote the revelations

O when that saint whom we call Bartholomew
he quickly joined Christ's band anew

O when that saint whom we call Peter
our hearts he always stirred

O when that saint whom we call James
he taught that Christ loves all the same

O when that saint whom we call Matthew
he was one of the closest few

O when that saint whom we call Philip
his hand with Christ he did dip

O when that saint whom we call Simon
for Christ he happily preached his sermon

O when that saint whom we call Thomas
beyond a doubt his faith guides us

My Soul Magnifies the Lord

My soul magnifies the Lord
my God, my Lord I adore

He is mighty
He has done great things for me

His name is holy
remember His mercy

He has scattered the proud
by His arm with strength endowed

He exalts the lowly
He dethrones the mighty

He has filled the hungry
He dismissed the rich empty

At your right hand
the queen in gold stands

Splendid is your robe
you reach around the globe

Shepherd
(Psalm 23)

The Lord is my shepherd
I shall not want
He makes me to lie down in green pastures

He leadeth me beside still waters
He restores my soul
He leads me in the paths of righteousness…for His namesake

Yea though I walk through the valley
of the shadow of death
I will fear no evil

For you are with me
your rod and staff they comfort me
you prepare a table for me

In the presence of my enemies
you anoint my head
with oil, my cup runneth over

Surely goodness and mercy
shall follow me
all the days of my life

And I will dwell
in the house of the Lord
for ever and evermore.

The Lord is my shepherd
I shall not want
He makes me to lie down in green pastures.

Joyful Noise
(Psalm 100)

Make a joyful noise to the Lord
all ye lands
serve the Lord with gladness
come before His presence with singing

Know that the Lord, He is God
it is He who has made us
not we ourselves, we are His people
and the sheep of His pasture

Enter His gates with thanks
into His courts with praise
be thankful to Him and bless His name
for the Lord is good.

His mercy is everlasting
and His truth endures
to all
generations
alleluia

The Lord Reigns
(Psalm 93)

The Lord reigns
He is clothed with majesty
the Lord is clothed
He has girded himself with strength

Surely the world is established
so that it cannot be moved
your throne is established from old
you're from everlasting

The floods have lifted up O Lord
the floods have lifted up their voice
the floods lift up, lift up their waves
the Lord on high is mightier

Than the noise of many waters
that the mighty waves of the sea
your testimonies are very sure

Holiness adorns
your house O Lord
for ever and ever

Amen